To all LGBTQIA youth

CHARACTERS:

EMMA- A quiet, unobtrusive high school student. She is open about her sexual orientation, but tries not to draw attention to herself.

KINSEY SCALE- A flamboyantly gay "Fairy Queen" who arrives to help Emma.This character can be portrayed by an actor of any gender, but Kinsey's characteristics fall into stereotypical gay male. However, where Kinsey comes from there's no such thing as a stereotype.

MS. SUPNIK- Emma's high school history class teacher. She is passionate about teaching history, but is not always aware of what's going on in the present.

RUDEPAUL- Drag version of RuPaul. Can be any gender. Part of the Gaggle of Gays who speak in rhyme.

ELLEN DEGENERATE- Drag version of Ellen Degeneres. Can be any gender. Part of the Gaggle of Gays who speak in rhyme.

AUDRE-LORDE-IT-OVER- Drag version of Audre Lorde. Can be any gender. Part of the Gaggle of Gays who speak in rhyme.

QUEERING HISTORY

Created by

MAGGIE KEENAN-BOLGER
AND THE YOUTH AT GREEN CHIMNEYS NYC DIVISION

Honest Accomplice Theatre

2014

Queering History- Edition #1 (2014)

Published by Maggie Keenan-Bolger as a part of Honest Accomplice Theatre

Cover design by Maggie Keenan-Bolger

Find out more about Honest Accomplice Theatre at honestaccomplice.org

A portion of play proceeds go to support LGBTQIA Homeless Youth.

ISBN: 978-1-312-05438-7

WALT WHITWOMAN- Drag version of Walt Whitman. Can be any gender. Part of the Gaggle of Gays who speak in rhyme.

OSCAR WILDER- Drag version of Oscar Wilde. Can be any gender. Part of the Gaggle of Gays who speak in rhyme.

JENNY- Pretty, popular cheerleader. Also, completely closeted.

CARSON- Outspoken, strong, trans-identified high school student. Closeted and pre-transition when not a part of Kinsey Scale's world.

BRANDON- Passionate, insightful high school student. Currently closeted. Played by an actor with disabilities.

JAVONNE- Proud, African-American, gay student. Currently closeted and well aware of the tensions among the cross-sections of identities within the LGBTQ communities.

DAVID HERO-TO- Ugandan gay rights activist David Kato. Incredibly brave, but in constant fear for his life. Though this character has a "drag name" he does not personify the camp or lightness of drag. He should be played as true to life as possible. His last name is pronounced as one fluid word, the last syllable sounds more like "toe" than "to," but we want to make sure we're not saying it as "hero toe."

DAVID B-HATE-I- Anti-gay rights activist and member of Ugandan Parliament, David Bahati. Truly believes that he is doing what is right. Can be any gender. Though this character has a "drag name" he does not personify the camp or lightness of drag. He should be played as true to life as possible.

RACHEL MAD-AS-HELL- Drag version of Rachel Maddow. Can be any gender. Though this character has a "drag name" she does not personify the camp or lightness of drag. She should be played as true to life as possible.

MANDERSON COOPER- Drag version of Anderson Cooper. Can be any gender. Though this character has a "drag name" he does not personify the camp or lightness of drag. He should be played as true to life as possible.

ANITA- Sassy, fun, proud student. Currently closeted, but unwilling to take crap from anyone.

Please Note: *All of these characters can be played by individuals of any gender. In fact, it is recommended the cast be as diverse as possible in regards to gender, sexual orientation, race, religion, age, ability, etc. The outlines above are only suggestions. Actors can also be double or triple cast.*

The reading of this script need not be word-perfect. The actors should feel free to adjust phrasing and words within reason to fit their particular voices.

LGBT History in 3 Minutes or Less written by Gena Oppenheim

Lights up on a high school history classroom. It should look like any other classroom. Posters with dead, white men on the walls, the Constitution, some grade "A" papers on bulletin boards and a diverse classroom of students. One or two students are relatively engaged, but most are bored out of their minds; some sleep, some giggle and pass notes in the back.

MS. SUPNIK, *the teacher, pulls out a large book with the title,* "The History of the World." *The students also have copies of the book on the desks in front of them. They begin to read...*

(The following lines are indicated by character, but need not be read "in character." They should be read as if the actors are playing themselves. This section needs to be rapid fire, each person almost interrupting the person before them.)

MS. SUPNIK: The year is...

WALT: 2001, 1963 –

ANITA: 1998, 1986 -

AUDRE: 1979, 1991 -

EMMA: *(Insert current year)*

MS. SUPNIK: The location? A High school classroom in…

The following lines are read with varied levels of enthusiasm.

CARSON: Knob Noster, MO. I got into all sorts of trouble there.

JENNY: Cleveland, Ohio. All girls Catholic school.

OSCAR: Laramie Wyoming...yes, *that* Laramie.

RUDEPAUL: Dallas, San Francisco, Salt Lake City, Albuquerque…

JAVONNE: Connecticut, Indiana, Arizona, Florida…

ELLEN: South Africa, China, Germany, The Philippines, Canada, England…

EMMA: New York City.

MS. SUPNIK: The subject? (*Joyfully, while she and the class open their books*) History!

MS. SUPNIK *is so thrilled and excited about the work she is doing she is completely oblivious to the boredom around her*

MS. SUPNIK: We're going to start on page 13 at the beginning of American history, with the great colonizer Christopher Columbus....

Light change.

EMMA: You hear all these stories about how bad high school was for gay kids. And, I dunno, it wasn't ever *good* for me, but it wasn't *bad* either. I was certainly not popular, I mean, I had people to sit with at lunch, but it's not like I ever felt like I could actually *tell* them anything about me. I was "out," yes, but not *too* out.

My favorite teacher that year was Ms. Supnik. She taught history and had such a passion for the stuff. You could see her, going off in her head to these things that happened way before any of us was alive. It was fun to see, but I wanted that connection too. None of the people she talked about were people I understood. They were all so old...and...stuffy...and....straight. Not that any of those things are bad, but I wanted to see people who looked like *me.* I mean, Ms. Supnik always said that history was supposed to show you how you *fit in* with the rest of the world. But I didn't know anything about people like me. So how could I fit in? What was the point? Where was *my* history?? How was I supposed to exist in the world if I didn't even know what being queer *looked* like?

> EMMA *slams her history book closed and it omits a cloud of dust. Fairy dust.* EMMA *coughs and tries to wave it away.*

MS. SUPNIK: In 1519, the first pandemic struck Hispaniola because of the diseases brought over by the Europeans.

> *As the fairy dust in* EMMA's *vision clears, she sees a man, with fairy wings and a wand, entering from the back of the house. He is*

accompanied by the Glinda entrance music from The Wizard of Oz. *On his way to the stage, he speaks to the audience.*

KINSEY: Excuse me, pardon me, ooooo, (*to a cute dude in audience*) hello sir!

MS. SUPNIK *is still teaching her lesson and everyone else seems totally unaware of the fairy in the classroom.*

MS. SUPNIK: A terribly fatal case of smallpox hit the Native American populations hard, killing 80-90% of the native people....

EMMA *is looking around frantically, trying to figure out why she seems to be the only one who sees this man in fairy wings coming towards her.*

EMMA: Um, I'm sorry, who are you?

KINSEY: Oh, hello Emma. I am, Kinsey Scale, the Fairy Queen and I am here to Queer. Your. History.

EMMA: Uh, okaaaay, but how do you know my name? And where did you come from?

KINSEY: Why Emma, don't you know? You summoned me! *(Pulls out a paper, clears throat and reads)* And I quote…'I don't know anything about people like me. So how can I fit in? What's the point? Where is *my* history?? How am I supposed to exist in the world if I don't even know what being queer *looks* like?' *(Folds up paper and puts it away)* You see? Classic Fairy Queen summoning.

EMMA: Okay, but, well…I appreciate your right to, um...be what...who...you are, but don't you think you could put…*(gesturing to wings)* those away? If my friends see you, I'm gonna end up dead.

KINSEY: Yes, Ms. Emma, I know, but don't think I just hopped out of bed this way, where I come from, these (*gesturing to wings*) take some serious dedication.

EMMA: *(dubiously)* Dedication?

KINSEY: Mm, hmm. I had to earn my fairy wings.

EMMA: Um, okay, but isn't that a little, uh...stereotypical?

KINSEY: Girl, where I come from, there's no such thing.

EMMA: Where *are* you from?

KINSEY: All in good time. But what matters here is you. I'm not here to embarrass you, in fact, I'm here to make your life just a little bit easier.

EMMA: You're here to help me? With what? Being gay?

KINSEY: Calm yourself my darling Lez-boo, before you get your boy briefs in a bunch, I've got some people I want you to meet. Ladies, gentlemen, and everyone in between, introducing my Gaggle of Gays! Maestro! Some music please!

The music changes to club music and the classroom is turned into a whirling, hopping drag show. When introduced, the GAGGLE OF GAYS *walk down the runway dancing and strutting in ways applicable to their time period and personality.* EMMA *is startled and thrilled to see her usually boring high school classroom utterly transformed.*

The members of the GAGGLE *are drag versions of historical characters and their genders are purposefully unstated. The actors can decide if they are playing male, female, somewhere along the spectrum or purposefully gender non-specific.*

KINSEY: First up, in our homo herd line up is the incomparable Walt Whitwoman. Born in 1819, Walt's sexuality has been widely disputed, but anyone who has read his famous poetry can read between the lines close enough to know he's one of us.

WALT WHITWOMAN *walks down the runway stroking his huge beard and waving to attractive, young gentlemen in the crowd.*

KINSEY: Then there's Oscar Wilder, Irish playwright known best for the public sodomy trial that tarnished his name and sharpened his wit. Don't let his marriage to Constance Lloyd fool you, he was guilty as sin.

OSCAR WILDER *struts down the runway, throwing green carnations to the crowd.*

KINSEY: Next up? Ms. Audre Lorde-It-Over. Black, lesbian, mother, warrior, poet. A self-defined multi-layered woman, don't you dare try to depict her as one thing, she's way more complex than you think.

AUDRE-LORDE-IT-OVER *walks down the runway, thoughtfully examining the audience, occasionally tipping her glasses down her nose to get a better look.*

KINSEY: The last two will be recognizable to our more..."contemporary" audiences. Ellen Degenerate and RudePaul have never shied away from the camera, gracing our TV screens with their super-gay brand of television fierce.

RUDEPAUL *and* ELLEN DEGENERATE *walk down the runway together,* RUDEPAUL *strutting and*

Vogueing, ELLEN *dancing just like she does on her show.*

KINSEY: Let's give it up for my Gaggle of Gays!

Wild applause as the GAGGLE *waves to the crowd before the lights dim and the classroom returns to normal.*

EMMA: You all came all this way just to teach me how to be gay?

KINSEY: Well, I'm not sure that's something that can be "taught" per se, but what exactly are you hoping for?

EMMA: I dunno. I just don't know how queer people are supposed to act, or dress, or *be*!

KINSEY: What? You want me to give you a pair of Birkenstocks and a guitar so that everyone can call you a lesbian?

EMMA: I don't know!!! You're the professional! You tell *me* what to do!

KINSEY: Well, okay, if you insist. Gaggle! Super Gay Symbol Supreme. Stat!

The GAGGLE *stands at attention.*

ELLEN: The Gaggle of Gays, all of, are we.

RUDEPAUL: RudePaul,

OSCAR: Wilder,

WALT: Whitwoman,

AUDRE: and me! Audre-Lorde-It-Over,

ELLEN: Ellen Degenerate,

WALT: We're here, we're queer, history we venerate.

RUDEPAUL: Perhaps you've noticed an unusual quirk,

OSCAR: We speak in rhyme, it's how we *work*.

AUDRE: We've heard you need some fashion aid,

WALT: Which is good, us gays? We've got it made.

ELLEN: First, a flannel to show them you are gay. Maybe, Doc Martens, cause then you're here to stay.

AUDRE: A thumb ring, so nice, a subtle sign out there.

And don't forget the asymmetrical hair.

OSCAR: A nautical star, tattooed on your left hand.

A turkey baster says you don't need a man!

RUDEPAUL: Green carnation, you're channeling Oscar Wilde.

Walt Whit? Poet, put calamus plant in style.

WALT: Then all the symbols: the lambda comes from Greek,

A purple hand or labrys you should seek.

AUDRE: A triangle, be it pink or purple or blue.

ELLEN: Some freedom rings around the neck for you.

OSCAR: A purple rhino, so docile, yet so fierce. For same-sex lovers, your right ear you will pierce.

RUDEPAUL: We top it off with a dose of rainbow flag.

With this get up, the ladies you will snag!

EMMA *is now awkwardly dressed in flags, symbols and ill-fitting clothing items. The* GAGGLE *stands around her, triumphant.*

KINSEY: There! The Super Gay Symbol Supreme! How do you feel?

EMMA: I feel like the Village People, Melissa Etheridge and Harvey Milk had a threesome that spawned a gender non-specific love child!

KINSEY: A remarkably accurate description. But was it what you were looking for?

EMMA: Not exactly.

KINSEY: (*sighs*) I didn't think so, the old "gay get-up" trick never works. It's nice, but doesn't exactly get to the core of the issue.

EMMA: Then what am I supposed to do now?

KINSEY: Never fear my little queer, I have a whole bag of tricks to pull from. All it takes is a little fairy dust and...

The student actors come back to life, sleeping, giggling.

MS. SUPNIK: …Now many of the traditions and values of the Native Americans were wiped out with the Europeans…

KINSEY *sprinkles the classroom with fairy dust.* MS. SUPNIK *breaks out of her history-induced trance and begins to look around. She sees* KINSEY, *the* GAGGLE *and* EMMA. *All of the students are shocked as well.*

MS. SUPNIK: Oh! Oh my! Such glitter! I...well, you don't look like my high schoolers, who are you? What are you doing here? Why are you in my history class?

KINSEY: Let's just say we're here to help. We're fellow historians if you will.

MS. SUPNIK: Fellow historians? Well, I love a good history lesson!

KINSEY: Well good, cause we're here to spice things up a little, give 'em a good shaking. To "queer" the usual methods...if you will.

MS. SUPNIK: Oh goody! Guest speakers! Please, please, go ahead.

KINSEY: Well, it just so happens that that little history book you seem so content to read out of could use a little something.

MS. SUPNIK: (*suddenly defensive*) My history book? What's wrong with it?! I've been teaching out of it for the last 20 years! It's remarkably accurate.

KINSEY: Accurate, maybe. Inclusive? Nuh uh. Why don't you just....hand it to me.

MS. SUPNIK: What?

Aghast, she holds the book to her chest like a child.

KINSEY: Hand. It. To. *Me*!

On the last syllable, KINSEY *sweeps the book out of* MS. SUPNIK's *tight grasp. Before the astonished* MS. SUPNIK *can say or do anything,* KINSEY *sprinkles it with fairy dust and it transforms into a brightly colored, sparkly version of* "The History of the World". *He then opens it to the front.*

KINSEY: Let's see...where to begin with? Ah, yes! Christopher Columbus sailed the ocean blue in 1492. Colonization...Native American traditions...ah ha! Here we are. Now! This is not a well-known fact, but one of the Native American traditions that was wiped out because of the Europeans was the Two-Spirit People.

MS. SUPNIK: Two-Spirit People?

KINSEY: Individuals who identified into a third gender role.

MS. SUPNIK: That's not in my history book!

KINSEY *hands her the book;* MS. SUPNIK *reads:*

MS. SUPNIK: Two-Spirit is an umbrella term sometimes used for what the disdainful Europeans referred to as berdaches. They wore clothes and performed work that was usually associated with both genders, male *and* female.

EMMA: (*bursts out*) Yes! That's it!

KINSEY: (*he knows what)* What?

EMMA: That's what this class is missing! We get to learn about all these straight, white guys, but there's never anyone like me.

KINSEY: (*innocently)* Like you?

EMMA: You know...

Embarrassed to say it loudly in front of everyone in the class.

KINSEY: Hmmmm??

EMMA: Like ME

KINSEY: *(Insert characteristics of Emma actress here)* Brunette? Female? 5 feet tall?

EMMA: No! *(Whispered)* Gay.

KINSEY: What?

EMMA: *(Loudly)* GAY!!

EMMA *is immediately embarrassed and looks around to see who heard.*

KINSEY: Ah, yes! Gay, queer, lesbian, Sapphist, fur trader, fister sister!

EMMA: ...right. All I want is to have the same, boring old facts taught about *gay* history that are taught about the presidents, and the wars and the goddamn Boston Tea Party! Is that too much to ask?

KINSEY *smiles and shrugs, turning to* MS. SUPNIK.

MS. SUPNIK: *(Regaining her composure)* I'm afraid I'm speechless. Perhaps my book *is* missing one or two things here and there.

KINSEY *nods knowingly.*

MS. SUPNIK: But regardless, boys and girls...

CARSON: And the rest of us!!

MS. SUPNIK: The rest of you?

CARSON: Yeah! The rest of us!

MS. SUPNIK: I'm sorry, I...

KINSEY *rolls his eyes and steps in.*

KINSEY: Yes, the rest of us. (*Whispers loudly to* MS. SUPNIK) Page 42.

MS. SUPNIK: Page 42? I...

KINSEY *points obviously to the sparkly book.* MS. SUPNIK *sees this and quickly turns to page 42. She is surprised, yet again, to see things in her book she's never seen before. She begins to read:*

MS. SUPNIK: Boys, girls, and those who identify as transgender, boi's with an "i", genderqueers, genderfuck, crossdressers, andros, unisex, pangender, bigender, agender, third gender, two-spirit, intersex, transexuals, en femme, girlfag, guydykes, sissies and those who wish not to identify themselves at this particular moment due to the fact that gender is an ever evolving and changing construct...*(big breath, looking up from the book, now at the end of the page)* It is now time for a pop quiz!

The students groan.

MS. SUPNIK: I'll just get these handed out and…

KINSEY: (*trying to stop her*) Oh!

MS. SUPNIK *freezes, confused.* KINSEY *attempts to indicate what he wants, but* MS. SUPNIK *doesn't understand and walks forward again.*

KINSEY: Eh!

Again MS. SUPNIK *freezes, this time annoyed. She looks at* KINSEY *who hums* "I'm Flying" *from* Peter Pan. MS. SUPNIK, *still confused, moves forward again.*

KINSEY: Bah!

MS. SUPNIK, *at this point, is questioning* KINSEY's *sanity. Frustrated,* KINSEY *finally resorts to acting out the scene of Tinkerbell's near death in* Peter Pan. *He does this in great detail with grandiose and dramatic gestures, playing the roles of Tinkerbell, Peter Pan and audience, encouraging himself to clap to indicate his own belief in fairies as he slowly and dramatically comes back to life. Once revived, he celebrates by prancing about the room throwing pretend fairy dust on everything he encounters.*

MS. SUPNIK *finally understands*

MS. SUPNIK: OH!

Realizing her mistake, MS. SUPNIK *holds out the papers to* KINSEY *who covers them in fairy dust.* MS. SUPNIK *smiles apologetically at him and hands out the papers to the students, who busily get to work.* EMMA *looks at her quiz.*

EMMA: Kinsey? *(He doesn't respond.)* Psst… Kinsey (KINSEY *is currently gazing into the audience, flirting with a cute boy*). KINSEY!!!

KINSEY: Hm? What? Oh! Yes! Yeeesss???

EMMA: I don't know the answers to any of these questions. Explain the "Marches on Albany." Who was Bayard Rustin? Draw a replica of the Mesolithic rock art in Sicily from 9660 to 5000 BC as it depicts phallic male figures in pairs that have been interpreted variously, including as depictions of homosexual intercourse. I'm sorry, *what*?!

KINSEY: Didn't you learn anything about LGBTQ History in the 12 years you've been in school?

EMMA: Um, I know about the Stonewall Riots....

KINSEY: Stonewall Riots?! Stonewall Riots?!?! How come the only thing anyone knows about LGBTQ history is the Stonewall Riots?!?!? Now, don't get me wrong, those were super important, as you can see they take up a whole chapter of our little "reformed" history book here. Let's see (*flips through it*), yes! Chapter 3; my sister Sylvia Rivera

REPRESENTED! Showing those pigs they couldn't fuck with us and our lives without some serious pushback. Now, that said, there is SO much more to our history than the dag gone Stonewall Riots! Gaggle of Gays! I think it's time for: A Brief Outline of LGBT History, In 3 Minutes or Less.

The GAGGLE *stands enthusiastically at attention. Throughout the piece, the Gaggle performs by switching costume pieces and deftly acting out the different characters. They have very clearly done this before and enjoy every second of it.*

ELLEN:

More than just letters,

LGBTQ,

So much history,

Is embedded in you.

OSCAR:

In 600 BC, Sappho of Lesbos wrote that:

Love is a limb-loosener that sweeps me away.

While Emperor Nero of Rome,

Had two husbands in his day.

His Countryman Julius Cesar might have asked for your ear,

But only wanted his beloved King Nicomedes near.

AUDRE:

Through the canons of antiquity,

More examples of LGBTQ love doth exist:

From Alexander the Great,

To even, some say, John the Baptist.

RUDEPAUL:

During the Italian Renaissance,

Much has been known,

About the love Da Vinci, Leonardo,

And other Ninja Turtles had shown.

But what of Sister Bendetta, who's fight with the Pope

Over her lover Sister Bartolema, gave others hope?

WALT:

And when the British Sun
Began its imperialistic Rise,
LGBTQ leaders were at the helm,
In many a guise.

AUDRE:

From Lady Boutler, who married Lady Hunt,
Then went on the lam.
To King James the 1st who knighted his lover,
The Earl of Buckingham.
Shakespeare dedicated Sonnet 126 to his groomsman, “Oh thou, My lovely Boy!”
And for nearly all his characters, cross-dressing brings them joy!

WALT:

Yes painters and Kings,
And famed writers too,
Are all part of the tapestry

woven by LGBTQ.

ELLEN:

Western Literature was indeed shaped,
By those who loved through closed doors.
Herman Melville wrote to Nate Hawthorne,
Your heart beats in my ribs and mine in yours.

RUDEPAUL:

Edna Saint Vincent Millay,
Marked of love in her day:
"She loves me all that she can,
And her ways to my ways resign;
But she was not made for any man,
And she never will be all mine."

OSCAR:

When the 20th century,
Began its trans-Atlantic flight,
LGBTQ figures stepped
Into the light.

AUDRE:

Emma Goldman preached in Union Square,
Bessie Smith sang notes no one had dared.
Alan Turing broke codes,
James Baldwin wrote odes,
Frida Kahlo painted vibrant visions,
GH Hardy revealed Nuclear fission.

RUDEPAUL:

Christine Jorgensen transitioned
In the public eye.
Hate crime laws were
Passed in Uruguay.

OSCAR:

Frank Kameny was the first
Out candidate in Washington DC.
While Sweden's the first
To offer free Hormone Therapy.

ELLEN:

And finally in 1973,

With pressure from every border.

The American Psychiatric Association

Removed Homosexuality as a "mental disorder."

WALT:

History is still being written,

So keep your pen close at hand.

There are many unjust laws

That still exist in this land.

AUDRE:

Because more than just letters,

LGBTQ,

So much history,

Is embedded in you.

Another student, CARSON, *who has been listening intently, pops out*

CARSON: Now hold on a sec, all that history is well and good, but history is *always* leaving people out.

EMMA: Wait! You aren't in my history class? Who are you?

CARSON: You know me Emma, I just look a little *different* now than I did back in high school.

EMMA: Different?

CARSON: More...masculine?

EMMA: (*has a light bulb moment)* Ooooo, yes! You...*(searching for the right word*)

CARSON: Transitioned? Yes, it's Carson now.

EMMA: Carson?! I...wow...(*doesn't know what to say*) congratulations....

CARSON: (*laughing kindly at Emma's obvious discomfort*) Thank you! It's not as shocking as it seems. I was trying my best to be as feminine as possible back then. Believe me, I'm much better at sports and math than I was letting on. (*To* KINSEY) Anyway, as I was saying, that sparkly book there, it's got the Greeks and Emma Goldman and Herman Melville. But what about the queers with disabilities? The people of color? The people from religious backgrounds who not only accept but *support* LGBTQ people or *are* LGBTQ themselves? We're not *just* gay you know, we have other identities too.

Another student, Brandon, *steps out.*

BRANDON: Carson has a point.

EMMA: Brandon, you're gay, too?!

BRANDON: I prefer the term queer but yes, me too.

A third student, JAVONNE, *steps forward.*

JAVONNE: Plus, LGBT "history," as well as our present, has *always* valued certain groups over others.

EMMA: Woah! You have got to be kidding me, we can't all be gay!

KINSEY: Times are a'changing my little fuzz bumper.

JAVONNE: There might be *more* of us, but that doesn't mean we've got stuff all worked out. If you want to look at history, check out the ways black people were systematically left out of the LGBT movement…

BRANDON: And people with disabilities…

CARSON: And trans people…

JAVONNE: Pretty much anyone seen as 'less acceptable' by straight people standards was conveniently ignored…

CARSON: Still are!

A white, preppy girl in a cheerleaders uniform, JENNY, *emerges from the students*

JENNY: Well, if we're going to talk about things that were ignored in our community, we need to talk about the AIDS crisis.

EMMA: Wait! WOAH! Hold on a sec. You're a *cheerleader*, you date a football player. There is *no way* you're gay.

JENNY: Oh Emma. Yes, I'm closeted now. But 15 years from now, you and I will see each other across a crowded bar in San

Francisco. Our matching asymmetrical haircuts drawing the other in, and it will only be hours later, after a blissful session of things far too marvelous to be recounted in mixed company, that we realize we went to high school together.

EMMA: (*squeaks*) I make out with *you*?! (*Whispers to* KINSEY) this is the best day of my life!

JENNY: This is the best day of your life *so far*...the real one is yet to come.

EMMA *is visibly thrilled.*

KINSEY: That's right Emma, you can't tell a gay book by its cover.

EMMA: (*Laughs, makes a joke for* JENNY'*s benefit*) Yeah, unless he's wearing fairy wings and carries pixie dust.

KINSEY: What? You think these wings say something about who I love? Oh no, honey, they don't call me Kinsey Scale for nothing.

EMMA: What's Kinsey Scale?

KINSEY: A scale of 0-6 with totally hetero on one side, and totally homo on the other. 1-5 are all the sexualities in between.

EMMA: Don't we just call those people bisexual?

KINSEY: Oh Emma, wouldn't it be nice if sexuality was that simple? Some people may be all the way on one end, some people may be all the way on the other, and yes, some may be smack dab in the middle. But most of us? We run between that 0 to 6 like Caster Semenya! *(Pauses for joke to land, but sees silence and blank looks)*…South African distance runner…subjected to gender testing… (*realizing no one knows who he's referring to*) …moving on...sexuality is so rarely static. I'll be a 6 one week....a 2 the next....let's just say I know each and every place on that scale *intimately*.

EMMA: You like *girls*?

KINSEY: And boys. And those who wish to identify as neither.

JENNY: Um, sorry to interrupt your little sexual fluidity conference here, but you *still* haven't talked about the AIDS crisis.

BRANDON: (*disappointed like he doesn't want to hear one more sad story about the AIDS crisis*) The AIDS crisis?

JENNY: Yes! Our history can be funny and campy, there's a lot of that, but it's not always so simple.

BRANDON: AIDS isn't just a gay thing you know, I'm tired of it being so tied to our community!

JENNY: Right, AIDS doesn't *only* affect gay people, but in the 80's...it hit our community the hardest.

KINSEY: She's right Brandon,

KINSEY *hands the book to* BRANDON.

KINSEY: Chapter 3, check it out.

Light change.

BRANDON: When I was a freshman in college I had finally come out of the closet. I was going through that super-gay phase where everything I did was uber-flamboyant, drawing as much attention to the fact that I was gay. I guess because I had hid it for so long I wanted to make my coming out EPIC. And it worked for a while. I found people like me, people who were as excited to be out as I was, and within a couple of months I started having sex with men for the first time. It was like this otherworldly experience. I'd spent so long fake smiling and grunting through sex with girls that the realization I could actually enjoy sex was not just a relief, it was bliss!

Then on November 7th, I still remember the date, I found a TIME magazine article about GRID. Gay Related Immune Deficiency. There had been rumblings about it among some of my friends, but I hadn't paid too much attention. I can remember being so excited to see something that was actually about gay people! Finally, we were being represented! Then I read the article. Turns out there was this disease that was killing us. People like me were getting deathly sick with an incurable illness that was being totally ignored by Ronald fucking Regan. There was this picture in the magazine of a Kaposi sarcoma lesion and my mind immediately went to a new mole I had just gotten on my stomach.

I freaked out. This mole, it meant I had AIDS. It meant I was sick and dying, too. I thought if I could just get it out of me, if I could make it go away, then I could somehow escape this thing, this killer. I don't really remember what happened next, but my roommate found me in the bathroom covered in blood. I had tried to cut the mole out of my stomach.

My roommate took me to the hospital and they patched me up.

After that I never got back the super pride and easy flamboyance from those first couple of months I was out. Maybe it's just cause I got older and wiser, maybe not.

But of all the introductions to the gay community, I wouldn't recommend that one to anyone.

Light change.

EMMA: But things have gotten better right? AIDS treatments are progressing, gay marriage is being legalized...

KINSEY: Well, maybe things are improving here, but we're only 5% of the world's population. There are still some places that have long way to go.

EMMA: What do you mean?

MS. SUPNIK: (*So happy to finally know something*) Oh! Oh! I think I know what you're talking about!

KINSEY: You do?

MS. SUPNIK: I'm not a total nincompoop you know, it's just hard when you have to stick with a curriculum...and, yes, it seems like my curriculum may be a teeny, tiny bit outdated.

KINSEY *gives her "a look."*

MS. SUPNIK: Or...wildly outdated. But I'm learning!

KINSEY: Well, well, Ms. Supnik, happy to hear you've come to your senses. By all means, please, share with the class.

MS. SUPNIK: I saw a news report about this just the other night. It was terrible, I could barely stay in front of my television...

Light change.

RACHEL: This is Rachel Mad-as-Hell.

MANDERSON: This is Manderson Cooper.

RACHEL: Reporting today from Uganda where Parliament is expected to vote tomorrow on a proposal intended to discourage homosexuality.

MANDERSON: The legislation would impose prison sentences, not only on gays and lesbians, but on those who fail to report homosexual behavior.

RACHEL: It also calls for the death penalty for some gay adults identified as, quote, "serial offenders."

MANDERSON: With me in the studio? David Hero-to.

RACHEL: David B-hate-i.

MANDERSON: David Hero-to is a Ugandan Gay Rights Activist.

RACHEL: David B-hate-i is the initiator of the 'Kill the Gays' bill and its strongest supporter in the Ugandan Parliament.

RACHEL AND MANDERSON: Thank you for joining me today.

HERO-TO: AND BA-HATE-I: My pleasure.

HERO-TO: I'm the very first gay man to be open in Uganda. I was closeted until I went to South Africa and discovered a gay Christian community there. They gave me hope, so I came back here to fight to liberate our people.

B-HATE-I: There are people coming into our country, recruiting children into homosexual behavior against their will. This is not an allegation, it's a fact.

HERO-TO: Not long after I came back, I was arrested and my brother said to me, 'David, you are alone. You have not discovered other gay people. You can't fight the battle alone.'

B-HATE-I: We believe that man was created to marry woman, and that's the purpose for which God created us.

HERO-TO: People began coming out to me. And now, the LGBT community brings us solidarity, a sense of belonging. We are friends, we are brothers, we are partners in the struggle.

B-HATE-I: I'm not involved in a hate campaign.

HERO-TO: Lesbians, they are being raped in an effort to make them heterosexual.

B-HATE-I: We are upholding family values.

HERO-TO: My mother should report me if this bill passes, my neighbor, my brother, otherwise they are imprisoned for three years. So, when you talk of the traditional family the bill is supposed to protect, I don't see the way it could.

RACHEL: If you make homosexuality punishable by life in prison, or in some cases by execution, what do you think will happen to gay people in Uganda?

B-HATE-I: We have conclusive research to the effect that homosexuality is a learned behavior and can be unlearned.

HERO-TO: If they pass this bill, no one will change, they will just go deeper into hiding. If we keep on hiding away, they will say we are not here.

MANDERSON: Aren't you afraid for your safety? Your life?

HERO-TO: If *I* run away, who will be left to defend the others?

Lights out on HERO-TO.

MANDERSON: Last week, a man was beaten to death with a hammer in his home. David Hero-to, the man who was killed, was one of the most outspoken activists for gay rights in his country.

B-HATE-I: The death of David Hero-to had nothing to do with the Kill the Gays bill.

MANDERSON: The local pastor leading the funeral service turned from eulogizing the man who'd been killed to instead railing against homosexuality.

B-HATE-I: It was a peaceful country before the invasion of homosexuality. We must now do whatever it takes to make it a peaceful country again.

RACHEL: David Hero-to's picture appeared on the cover of a local paper as somebody who ought to be hanged for being gay.

B-HATE-I: What happened was a robbery, nothing more.

MANDERSON: Hero-to received numerous death threats in the months leading up to his attack.

B-HATE-I: Maybe a personal disagreement, we should not over blow the death of one man.

RACHEL: The parliament, police force and David B-hate-i *insist*, the murder of this openly gay man had *nothing* to do with the "Kill the Gays" bill.

Light change.

EMMA: Why would you show me that? I thought it was gonna be some great story about overcoming triumph. And then he died! A person who was doing the right thing got killed! And the stupid guy in Parliament tried to make it seem like it was the gays' fault for making things violent instead of the government's fault for raping, attacking and killing the gays. It's not fair!

KINSEY: Listen Emma, I know it's hard, but it's a part of our history. Just because it's not pretty doesn't mean it shouldn't be told. (*Sighs*) Listen, you asked me where I was from before and, well, it's kind of hard to explain. But let's just say...I get you. Trust me, all the fabulousness and sass you see before you was lost on most of my emphatically breeding classmates in high school. There is *nothing* more threatening than a radical feminist gay boy with killer fashion sense.

EMMA: So, what, you got beat up?

KINSEY: Yep. Beat up, tormented, and more. Eventually the kids in my school decided they'd do better without me there to question their masculinity.

EMMA: (*horrified*) They killed you?

KINSEY: Not a pretty story I know, but something good did come of it. For every act of homophobic bullying, violence and murder, a queer fairy gets his wings. It's how the universe balances things out. For every bad, ignorant thing that goes on, something fabulously fierce is produced.

EMMA: Is that why you are the (*gesturing vaguely to* KINSEY) *way* you are?

KINSEY: Are you referring to my gait? My fashion choices? My "flamboyance" if you will?

EMMA *nods.*

KINSEY: As a queer kid you only get one impression of what gay men are like. And this was my impression. I would have given my favorite Gucci purse to be able to live *this* way and be *this* person in high school. Since I couldn't back then? I do it now. What *you* call a stereotype, *I* call making up for lost time.

EMMA: Wow. Well, you'd think we'd stop needing you guys. I mean, there's anti-bullying legislation most places, people here get in trouble when they beat up other kids.

KINSEY: Being hurt as a queer kid doesn't just mean getting beat up. There's a lot more to it than that.

BRANDON: Like teachers ignoring gay slurs or comments. Or even using them themselves.

CARSON: Like being forced to dress in the "women's locker room" or the "men's locker room" or line up according to "boy" or "girl."

JENNY: Like not being able to touch your friends because then everyone will think that *they're* gay too.

Another student steps forward, ANITA. *She's been flipping furiously through the queered history book and holds it up to show the other students the chapter she's found.*

ANITA: Like kids failing out of school because they've been kicked out for coming out. And not having systems to give them safe, happy places to go.

Light change.

ANITA *reads from the book.*

ANITA: Each night in New York City, a minimum of 3,800 youth are homeless, more than half of whom identify as lesbian, gay, bisexual or transgender.

BRANDON: LGBT youth who are rejected by their families are more than 8 times as likely to attempt suicide...

EMMA: Nearly 6 times as likely to report high levels of depression....

JAVONNE: And are more than 3 times as likely to be at high risk for HIV and STI's than their peers who were more accepted by their families.

CARSON: My family was incredibly tight-knit, we did everything together. We never had much money, but we would take trips to the beach just outside the city, put blankets together and spent all summer eating peanut butter sandwiches and wading in the ocean.

My mom got sick when I was 10 and everything changed. We stopped going to the beach and my dad had to work three jobs to pay the hospital bills.

I was the one who took care of my sisters mostly and they *hated* it. We would have screaming matches about who was supposed to take out the garbage, do the dishes or clean up the lawn.

Mom died when I was 13. Once she was gone, our home turned into a boot camp, my dad wouldn't let any of us do anything but go to school and church. Church was the worst. He'd yell at me to put on a dress, I'd ignore him. He'd yell more, ask me what the big fucking deal was, it was a dress, every other girl was wearing them. I would just stare at him not answering.

He thought I was being stubborn by not answering, but really, I had no idea myself. I had never met a trans person before, had no idea that we even existed. So all I knew was that there was something wrong with me. *And* that I did not want to wear that goddamned dress.

I came out to him as a lesbian and he told me that I was going to burn in hell. Told me he couldn't have me in the house with my sisters and told me to find someplace else to stay.

I couch-hopped with friends for a while till I couldn't stand it anymore. Eventually I found a guy who took me in. It was better than being on the streets, but he made it pretty clear I had to have sex with him if I wanted to stay. So I did.

I missed my sisters. I was worried my Dad wouldn't know how to cut Lilia's sandwiches into birdies so she would eat them at lunch, or that Lauren still needed her stuffed cow to get to sleep at night. I tried to catch them before they went into school sometimes, but he'd obviously told them something so they wouldn't talk to me. And they didn't.

It was on the streets that I first met other trans kids. I had been out as a lesbian for a while, but it still felt wrong and uncomfortable. I used to watch the other trans guys from afar to see how they did it. Finally I got up the courage to talk to one of them. I begged him to help me out. I must have drove him nuts because finally, after making sure that, yes, this was what I *really* wanted, he gave me my first binder for my chest, and taught me the tricks for how to pack in a way that didn't just look like balled up socks in your pants.

I took to it pretty quick, but the guy I was living with hated it. Told me if he wanted a faggot to sleep with he would have found one. So I had to leave. I tried the shelters, but those were even worse. They made me stay in the women's section and every time I walked in I could feel the women glaring at me, what was this twink doing in *their* area? People in the shelters have a lot of aggression they need to take out on somebody. I was the 90-pound kid in boys' clothes, an easy target.

After a couple of months, I was one of the few kids allowed into a homeless program just for LGBT youth. My life wasn't magically fixed, but at least I could stop watching my back for two seconds, stop worrying about getting beat up and focus on getting my life back together. That place saved me.

No one expects us to amount to anything really, but I managed to get out of the system. I've got a job now, a partner.

Two weeks ago I got a phone call. I didn't recognize the number, but I picked up anyway and it was my sister. I could tell she was scared to talk to me, but I was so glad to hear her voice.

I'm still real angry with her and my dad and everything. But, just the fact that she called meant so much. I told her about my transition and I still don't think she agrees with my "lifestyle," but we're meeting for coffee tomorrow. I'm terrified (*after a moment of thought*) and excited.

This section can be updated with current and/or local statistics about LGBT *Homeless Youth.*

BRANDON: With over 3,800 homeless youth on the streets in NYC each night, there are only 250 shelter beds available.

EMMA: For the 1,600 LGBT youth, only 42 of those beds are offered in LGBT-specific shelters.

JENNY: In the past two months, Green Chimneys, one of the first child welfare agencies for LGBT homeless youth, had to shut down their transitional independent living program and move their Bronx office to a smaller, less expensive space.

CARSON: LGBT youth homelessness isn't pretty, and it's not fun, but it's real. *We're* real. If our community could put as much effort into supporting *us* as they do in supporting gay marriage, maybe we could make some progress. Not saying marriage isn't important, but, ya know, it just seems secondary to finding a place to call home.

Light Change

ANITA: Yes. This is all so true, and important, but you're killing me with the dramatics! What about the JOY of being LGBT, what about the fierceness in our community, the tenacity of our people!

EMMA: Yes! Thank you Anita, I get why this is needed, but it's not making me want to be any more "out." I mean, I would rather not have to go back into the closet to protect myself cause I'm as "free" as you were...*(to* KINSEY*)* no offense.

KINSEY: None taken my little Sapphoholic. And yes, it can be dangerous to be out. It scares people, and in some places it can be fatal. It's not for everyone, some queer kids have to wait till they're out of the house, or out of their school to come out. But that doesn't mean they need to be closeted to *themselves*. Sometimes, being closeted can be just as dangerous as the alternative.

ANITA: We're also stronger than we think we are. *I've* got people pushing me down every day because of how I look and who I love. But I can't let it bother me. Cause you know what? I know who I am, and I know what *I* can do.

EMMA: Yeah. It seems like we need to stop worrying about what other people think and just be who we are.

KINSEY: I'm sorry, what was that last thing you just said?

EMMA: We need to stop worrying about what other people think and just be who we are?

KINSEY: Ah, so simple a solution, so difficult in practice.

EMMA: Is that why you chose me? To show me how to "be who I am?"

KINSEY: Partially, yes. And in some ways it was just the luck of the draw. Not everyone is as lucky as you, most LGBTQI...LMNOP kids go through their lives never realizing the people who came before them. If they *are* lucky enough to figure it out, they spend the rest of their lives wishing they'd known it earlier. But with great knowledge comes great responsibility. Speaking of which, Ms. Supnik, what's the next chapter in this lovely little history book of ours?

Now teaching from this book like it was her old one, excited to be sharing the information.

MS. SUPNIK: Learning from your past. If you were to give advice to your younger self what would it be?

EMMA: If I was to give advice to my younger self?

Light change. Again, these lines don't need to be spoken "in character"

EMMA: If I was to give advice to my younger self...

OSCAR: People who care too much about your sexuality or gender really ought to have other things to do.

RUDEPAUL: Being gay is your superpower.

JAVONNE: Someday you'll look back and say, "I'm a fucking champ for getting through this shit!"

OSCAR: What made you weird in high school will make you bank when you graduate.

AUDRE: Don't be afraid to say no. Don't be afraid to say yes.

MS. SUPNIK: Fuck a lot in high school.

ELLEN: Act your age, be a kid, have fun. It's not that serious.

WALT: The guys on the football team are not as straight as they seem.

CARSON: Stay in San Francisco.

JENNY: Get the hell out of Texas.

JAVONNE: It's not impossible.

AUDRE: Stop dieting. My God, life is too short to be hungry over 5 pounds.

CARSON: Yes, transitioning is totally right for you.

WALT: Go into therapy *much* sooner.

ANITA: Keep fighting.

JENNY: Life it too short to not make out with the cute cheerleader.

CARSON: Even if you were born into a terrible situation, the fact that you are alive means you can experience better things.

MS. SUPNIK: Talking all the time is not the same as being funny.

ANITA: We're *not* just the tragic stories you hear on the news.

ELLEN: Start working out now.

BRANDON: Your AIDS diagnosis is not the end of the world. There are some amazing medical advancements in the mix. Don't give up hope.

RUDEPAUL: The rainbow has room for grey areas!

JAVONNE: Don't take what people *say* about the Bible as the only truth. It's about love, not hate.

ELLEN: Everybody already knows.

JENNY: Don't kiss so many boys on your way to self-discovery.

RUDEPAUL: You don't have to like other gay people *just* because they're gay.

CARSON: Be your *own* hero.

JAVONNE: You will be a part of a movement far greater than anything your boring, white, straight friends will ever get to experience.

WALT: Cut off all your hair and start reading more Feminist literature. You enormous homosexual.

OSCAR: You ended up very lucky, but wear a condom.

MS. SUPNIK: Don't be ashamed when everyone makes fun of you because your two girl dolls share a bed. It made sense to you, go with it.

BRANDON: I don't think I have any advice. But it's probably for the best. I know how much my younger self hated being told what to do.

Light change

KINSEY: Well, I'm afraid it's about that time...

EMMA: What time?

KINSEY: Time for me to sashay...away

EMMA: What? But wait!! You just started! (*Frantically*) There's so much more to think about, to talk about!!! What about Hispanic gay rights? The Firehouse? Proposition 8!! You can't have a gay history lesson without talking about Proposition 8!

KINSEY: Well you can't expect me to cover everything gay under the sun in a mere hour and fifteen minutes!

EMMA: But that's not fair! I want to know! There's no one else who is going to tell me this stuff!

KINSEY: Maybe not directly, but it's all around you.

EMMA: (*near to tears*) Oh, so you expect me to get through high school just looking at *subtext*?!?! You can't just throw these things at me and leave me hanging!

KINSEY: Listen, I understand. It's hard now, but...

EMMA: What? It gets better? Yeah, that's what all they say. And that's nice for 10 years from now when it actually *is* better, but what about *now*?! What am I supposed to do *now*?!?!

KINSEY: Emma. Stop. You're stronger than you think. And your community is out there, I promise. You're not the only person sitting in your high school class wishing for something more, something better. Just look around you.

CARSON *takes* EMMA's *hand*

CARSON: I'm here.

JENNY: Me too.

JAVONNE: We all are. We're not out yet, but we get it. And we look up to you.

EMMA: To me?

BRANDON: Right now? In high school? You're already what I can only dream of becoming.

CARSON: You're changing people without even knowing it, just by being you.

ELLEN: It's hard we know, your peers, they may seem few

OSCAR: But stand on our shoulders.

RUDEPAUL: Cause our history? It's in you.

JENNY: And when things get really rough, remember. In 10 years, you're going to have a night neither of us will ever forget.

KINSEY: And at that, I must go. Oh look! My bubble is here!

EMMA: Bubble? Like in the Wizard of Oz? You've got to be kidding me.

KINSEY: I never kid, kid. Just remember, our history is in you.

STUDENTS/TEACHER/GAGGLE (*like the Munchkins from the Wizard of Oz*) Goodbye! Goodbye!

> KINSEY *gets into his bubble, which, yes, does oddly resemble Glenda's in* The Wizard of Oz. *Lights change as* KINSEY *flies offstage, throwing fairy dust all over everything, returning it to its previous state. The students and teacher go back to their original positions. The students sleep and giggle.* MS. SUPNIK *closes the queered history book. When she re-opens it, it's lost its sparkle. The only thing not back to normal, it seems, is* EMMA.

MS. SUPNIK *is nearing the end of her lesson for the day.*

MS. SUPNIK: …so those are all of the things the Native American culture lost because of the arrival of Christopher Columbus.

EMMA: (*bursts out, surprising herself and everyone in class*) What about the Two-Spirit People?

MS. SUPNIK: The what?

EMMA: (*now nervous*) The Two Spirit People...they fulfilled mixed gender roles...(*trails off, realizing what she's done*)

At the mention of this, CARSON, *now pre-transition perks up. As do the rest of the students in the class.*

CARSON: (*trying to be nonchalant but is clearly desperate to know)* Mixed gender roles?

EMMA: Yeah, ya know...

EMMA *looks around for* KINSEY, *hoping for help. Not seeing him, she looks pleadingly at the other queer students only to see that they are hanging on to her every word. All except for* JENNY *who looks uncomfortable, clearly wanting to cover up her own sexuality.*

JENNY: (*disdainful)* Pfft, mixed gender roles? What is this? Some dyke vendetta?

MS. SUPNIK: Now hold on Jenny, I don't care who it applies to, it's a part of our history. And I believe the term you're looking for is "lesbian" not "dyke." Please go on Emma, this sounds incredible, I can't believe it's not in the book!

EMMA: *(Takes a deep breath, starts off rocky, but gets more confident*) Well, they wore clothes and performed work that was usually associated with both genders, male *and* female. And they were *totally* accepted into their communities, in fact, it was a really important part of how they worked. They've been documented in a whole bunch of the tribes....

Lights slowly fade with EMMA *explaining Two-Spirit People to the class.* MS. SUPNIK *is thrilled to see someone else as excited about history as she is.*

BRANDON, CARSON, ANITA *and* JAVONNE *are listening intently, hanging on to* EMMA's *every word. And in the corner, we see* JENNY, *in her cheerleaders outfit, slowly, but surely, falling in love.*

www.ingramcontent.com/pod-product-compliance
Ingram Content Group UK Ltd.
Pitfield, Milton Keynes, MK11 3LW, UK
UKHW021050270726
13967UKWH00012B/60

9 781312 054387